NOSTALGIC VIEWS OF
GETTYSBURG

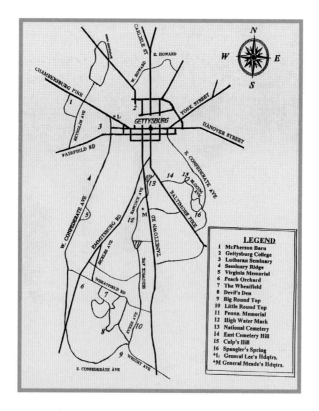

NOSTALGIC VIEWS OF

GETTYSBURG

Library of Congress control number: 2005933192

Published by Arcadia Publishing for Borders Group, Inc.
Visit us on the internet at www.arcadiapublishing.com

CONTENTS

INTRODUCTION

During the spring of 1863 the small town of Gettysburg, with a population of 2,400, was best known as the seat of Adams County, Pennsylvania and as the home of the Lutheran Theological Seminary and a small college. Most people outside south central Pennsylvania were probably unfamiliar with this rural community only eight miles from the famed Mason Dixon line. This relative anonymity was to change forever in early July of that fateful year.

The Civil War had been going on for two years when Gen. Robert E. Lee, commander of the Confederate Army of Northern Virginia, decided to take the war to the Northern states. With the capture of Harrisburg, Pennsylvania, as an objective, Lee and his formidable army marched north through the Pennsylvania countryside in June 1863. The Union Army of the Potomac, which would soon be under command of Gen. George G. Meade, was approaching from the south and east. Although not the initial choice of either army for the site of a conflict, fate would have it that these two massive forces would converge on this small town on July 1. The resulting battle involved fighting that took place over approximately 25 square miles of terrain in and around the town. Before it was over, more than 172,000 soldiers engaged in combat. During July 1, 2, and 3, in what has become known as the Battle of Gettysburg, an estimated 51,000 men were killed, wounded, captured, or recorded as missing. Thus Gettysburg became the location of the largest and bloodiest battle ever fought on American soil. The events that occurred here would culminate in the "high tide" of the Confederacy and mark the turning point of the Civil War.

It is said that Gettysburg is one of the most written-about and analyzed conflicts in history. The purpose of this book is to present the battle's dramatic story in a unique and hopefully interesting manner, through the use of vintage postcards published from 1900 through the early 1920s. These images portray both the town and the major events of the battle, as well as many of the monuments erected in Gettysburg National Military Park.

For the benefit of postcard collectors, the name of the publisher, card number, and the date or estimated date of publication is included, when known. Postcards have long been utilized as souvenirs or as an easy way to send a quick message; they are also useful as snapshots of history.

Those who visit the battlefield will surely notice that many of the scenes depicted on these postcards have changed. But one thing has remained the same over the decades, no matter the view—the battlefield stands as a tribute and lasting remembrance to all those, from the North and South, who fought here in the summer of 1863.

ONE

THE TOWN

H. S. Huidekoper's relief map of Gettysburg clearly shows how the ten major roads leading into town looked much like the spokes of a wheel. Because of these converging routes, and the fact that the town lay in the paths of the Army of the Potomac and the Army of Northern Virginia, the town of Gettysburg was destined to become the site of the Civil War's greatest battle. (W. H. Tipton, #219; c. 1901.)

BATTLEFIELD OF GETTYSBURG.

AS IT WAS IN 1863.

1. Emmitsburg Road.
2. Millerstown Road.
3. Hagerstown Road (Fairfield)
4. Chambersburg Pike (Cashtown)
5. Mummasburg Road.
6. Carlisle Road.
7. Harrisburg Road.
8. Hunterstown Road.
9. York Pike.
10. Hanover Road.
11. Baltimore Pike.
12. Taneytown Road.

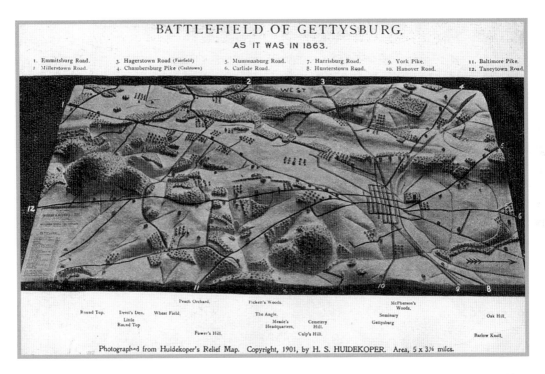

Round Top.
Devil's Den.
Little Round Top.
Wheat Field.
Peach Orchard.
Power's Hill.
Pickett's Woods.
The Angle.
Meade's Headquarters.
Cemetery Hill.
Culp's Hill.
McPherson's Woods.
Gettysburg
Seminary
Oak Hill.
Barlow Knoll.

Photographed from Huidekoper's Relief Map. Copyright, 1901, by H. S. HUIDEKOPER. Area, 5 x 3½ miles.

11

Founded in 1780 by James Gettys, for whom the town was named, Gettysburg consisted of approximately 450 buildings and had a population of 2,400 in 1863. As the county seat of Adams County, the town also boasted a Lutheran Seminary and a small college. Here the town can be seen to the south of what is now North Confederate Avenue. (W. H. Tipton, multiview set; c. 1905.)

8/7/5

GETTYSBURG, Pa. GENERAL VIEW OF THE BATTLEFIELD.

Penrose Myers, Gettysburg, Pa.

Our "Jolly Eight" drove here this morning. We have been over the battlefield. Tomorrow we break camp & return home. Yours
Walt Wardbrook

CENTER SQUARE, GETTYSBURG, PA.

14

Like many small Pennsylvania towns, Gettysburg possesses a center square into which four major streets converge. On July 1, 1863, Union troops of the 1st and 11th Corps fled through this town center on their way to Cemetery Hill, to the south. Fighting was to occur here and along the streets and alleys as Union soldiers were driven down Baltimore Street. (David Kaufman, #102527: c. 1915.)

Running north from the center square, Carlisle Street is one of the four major thoroughfares in town. On the first day of battle it served as one of the routes by which Confederate troops entered Gettysburg and along which Union soldiers fled. (W. H. Tipton, #209; *c.* 1908.)

This railroad station, located on the corner of Washington and Railroad Streets, was built by the Gettysburg & Harrisburg Railroad in 1884. The station was built to help increase accessibility for tourists coming to visit the nearby battlefield. (Union News Co., #1151; c. 1910.)

RAILROAD STATION, GETTYSBURG, PA.

MAIN STREET, GETTYSBURG, PA.

EAGLE HOTEL

This view of busy Chambersburg Street shows the Eagle Hotel. Even in 1863, this street was home to a number of businesses. On the first day of battle, the Southern forces approaching from the west entered the town by way of this street. (Union News Co., #1137; c. 1910.)

Located along Baltimore Street, this house, known formerly as the "Sweeney House," was occupied by Confederate sharpshooters during the battle. Numerous bullet and shell holes still remain in the building. For years the home was owned by the Black family, who rented rooms to tourists. It is now restored and known as the Farnsworth House Inn. (Louis Kaufmann & Sons; c. 1910.)

THE HOME OF GEORGE P. BLACK, GETTYSBURG, PA., COMMONLY KNOWN AS THE « SWEENEY HOUSE »

GETTYSBURG COLLEGE, SHOWING ALL THE BUILDING, GETTYSBURG, PA.

Established in 1832, Gettysburg College is the oldest Lutheran College in America. Originally part of the Lutheran Theological Seminary, it was known as Pennsylvania College in 1863. During and after the battle most of its buildings served as hospitals for the many wounded. (Louis Kaufmann & Sons, #36; c. 1907.)

Milton Valentine Hall is one of several buildings comprising the Lutheran Theological Seminary, which is located on the west end of town. This institution, one of the town's most noted features in 1863, gave the name Seminary Ridge to this locale. During the battle and for months after, these buildings were to serve as hospitals for the many wounded of both armies. (W. H. Tipton, multiview set; c. 1905.)

LUTHERAN THEOLOGICAL SEMINARY BUILDINGS

W.H. TIPTON PHOTO

TWO

DAY ONE

Statues of Gen. Buford, Gen. Reynolds and Hall's 2nd Maine Battery, Gettysburg, Pa.

At approximately 8:00 a.m. on July 1, 1863, two brigades of dismounted Union cavalry commanded by Gen. John Buford engaged two advancing brigades of Confederate infantry of Gen. Henry Heth's Division. This initial encounter on McPherson's Ridge was soon to escalate into the largest battle of the Civil War. The cannon mounted at the base of Buford's statue are the very ones which fired the first Union artillery rounds of the conflict. (C. T. Photochrom, #R-37856; c. 1913.)

Early in the battle, around 10:00 a.m., Union Gen. John F. Reynolds was shot and killed while directing his troops at the edge of McPherson's Woods (since renamed Reynolds' Woods). Shortly after, General Meredith, leading the "Iron Brigade," attacked through the woods, successfully putting to flight Confederate troops under command of Gen. James Archer. Nearly 1,000 prisoners were taken, including General Archer. (J. I. Mumper; 1909.)

First Days Fight Reynolds Woods.
Gettysburg, Pa.

AT THE MC PHERSON BARN, GETTYSBURG.

34

The 150th Pennsylvania Volunteer Infantry, known as the "Bucktail" Brigade, is shown behind a split-rail fence attempting to repel a Confederate attack. After suffering extremely high casualties, they were driven from the battlefield. The barn was later to be used as a hospital. (Rotograph Co., #E-3720a; c. 1907.)

The McPherson barn, situated along the Chambersburg Pike, was the scene of intense fighting. This postcard depicts the afternoon attack by Confederate troops of Col. John Brockenbrough's Virginian Brigade. The Confederates were successful in driving away the Pennsylvania Bucktails, who were defending the barn and its surrounding ground. (A. C. Bosselman & Co., #13008; c. 1910.)

The Storming of the Barn on the McPherson farm.

John L. Burns' Home and his Statue, Gettysburg, Pa.

Copyright by W. H. Tipton.

38

Upon hearing the sounds of battle, John Burns, a citizen reputed to have been over 70 years of age, took up his gun to help repel the rebel attackers. He joined the skirmishing line of the 150th Pennsylvania Regiment, and later that day, the 2nd Wisconsin. He was wounded three times before the day was finished. Burns became known as the "Hero of Gettysburg" for his actions. In this picture, from a photograph taken in July 1863, Burns is on the porch of his home recovering from his wounds. In later years he served as the town's constable. Death finally claimed him in 1872, and he is now buried in Evergreen Cemetery. (W. H. Tipton, #5875; c. 1915.)

This view along Howard Avenue shows the relatively flat ground where the Union 11th Corps defended their battle line until about 3:30 p.m. Around that time the Union line broke and the Confederate army drove them through town and back to positions on Cemetery Hill. (W. H. Tipton, #302; c. 1910.)

General Robert E. Lee and Staff,
Gettysburg, Pa.

Son of Revolutionary War hero "Lighthorse" Harry Lee, Gen. Robert E. Lee was appointed commander of the Army of Northern Virginia on June 1, 1862. He remained an idolized and beloved leader of his army even after his defeat at Gettysburg. Shown here mounted on "Traveller," his famous iron-gray horse who carried him throughout the war, Lee arrived on the battlefield late in the afternoon. By that time the Union 1st and 11th Corps had been routed and were reorganizing on Cemetery Hill. Confederate lines stretched in a semicircle about six miles to the north and west, while the Union army consolidated its defensive line in the shape of a fishhook about three miles long. (C. T. Photochrom, #R-37844; c. 1913.)

This small, picturesque stone farmhouse constructed in 1779, the home of the widow Mary Thompson, was where General Lee made his headquarters throughout the battle. It is near the crest of Seminary Ridge and fronts directly on the Chambersburg Pike (now U.S. Route 30), within sight of the Lutheran Seminary. The general himself actually slept in a tent pitched nearby. Today the building houses the General Lee's Headquarters Museum. (Union News Co., #M-3111; c. 1910.)

General Lee's Headquarters, Chambersburg Pike, Gettysburg Battlefield, Pa.

45

General Meade's Headquarters, Gettysburg, Pa.

Very late on the night of July 1, Gen. George Meade arrived from Taneytown, Maryland and established his headquarters in this tiny farmhouse, which was only 16 by 20 feet square. It was from here, the home of the widow Mrs. Leister, that Meade directed his army on the second and third days of the battle. On the third day, the general and his staff were forced to evacuate the house because of the intense cannonade prior to Pickett's Charge. The bombardment was so severe that 27 horses of his headquarters guard were killed at this site. (C. T. Photochrom, #R-37842; c. 1913.)

THREE

DAY TWO

On the second day of combat General Meade utilized 210 of his regiments in order to firm up and defend his positions. General Lee used 86 regiments in attacking both flanks of the Union Line. Some of the heaviest fighting of the day took place over the landscape seen in this view. (Rotograph Co., #G-3712; 1904.)

Copyright 1904 by the Rotograph Co.

G 3712 General view from little Round Top, looking across the Valley of Death to the wheat field, Statue of Gen. Warren in foreground, Gettysburg, Pa.

Had a long drive this morning. Carroll.

General Geo. G. Meade and Corps Commanders at Gettysburg, Pa.

This reproduction of an authentic U.S. War Department photograph shows Gen. George Meade and his staff. Meade assumed command of the Army of the Potomac on June 28, 1863, little realizing that the decisions he would make and actions he would take in just a few days would ultimately determine the outcome of the Civil War. (A. C. Bosselman & Co., #13000; c. 1910.)

Signal Rock was the location of the Union Army's first occupation of Little Round Top. From here the signal corpsmen observed enemy movements below and communicated this information to other Federal positions. It was while visiting this station that Gen. G. K. Warren saw the need to immediately fortify these heights before they could be captured by Confederate forces. Warren hastily ordered two elements of the 5th Corps, Vincent's Brigade, and Lieutenant Hazlett's artillery battery to secure the high ground. These troops reached the summit only minutes before a Confederate assault by General Law's Alabamians. For his quick action General Warren is remembered as "the savior of Little Round Top." (American News Co., #A-6608; c. 1907.)

Signal Rock on Little Round Top looking North to Scene of Pickett's Charge. Gettysburg, Pa.

Confederate infantry crossed here between the roundtops on their way to storm the heights of Little Round Top. The 83rd Pennsylvania Regiment rushed in to try to halt the attack. Its commander, Col. Strong Vincent, was killed at a spot only a short distance behind where this monument now stands. Only the timely arrival of the 140th New York Regiment helped to break up the assault. (W. H. Tipton, #210; c. 1908.)

Devil's Den,
Gettysburg, Pa.

216926

58

On the west side of the Valley of Death and just below Little Round Top, Devil's Den, a natural fortification of large rocks and crevices, was briefly held by Union soldiers. After capture by General Hood's Confederates, the area was utilized as a sniper's nest, as it afforded natural protection and a clear view of the summit of Little Round Top. Confederate sharpshooters hidden among the boulders were responsible for numerous casualties of the Union officers and soldiers atop Little Round Top. Among those killed before nightfall on July 2 were brigade commander Gen. Stephen Weed and artilleryman Lt. Charles Hazlett. The Confederates kept possession of the rocky roost until their retreat at the end of the battle. (Leighton & Valentine , #216926; c. 1913.)

After being driven from Devil's Den and the surrounding area, Union troops fought courageously on the marshy flatland at the base of Little Round Top, which was to be named the Valley of Death. The small creek, Plum Run, which flows through the center of this view, ran red with the blood of countless dead and wounded and thus became known as "Bloody Run." (A. C. Bosselman & Co., #11729; c. 1910.)

Valley of Death and Little Round Top, Gettysburg, Pa.

61

On the evening of July 2, Confederate soldiers of Johnson's Brigade attacked Culp's Hill, successfully capturing the breastworks at the base of the hill. They were to hold these positions until the next morning. From nearby Stevens Knoll, Union artillery poured a devastating enfilading fire on the enemy as they attempted an assault on East Cemetery Hill. (W. H. Tipton, #306; c. 1910.)

As evening began to fall, units of the Confederate "Louisiana Tigers" charged the fortifications at the base of East Cemetery Hill, breaking through the Union line. After driving their foe up the slope, they captured the hill just as darkness fell. Their victory was brief however, as Federal reinforcements from Hancock's 2nd Corps arrived and repulsed their attack. The Louisiana Tigers were driven back down the slope in fierce hand-to-hand combat. Union artillery fire from nearby Stevens Knoll also took a toll on their numbers. By the time the fighting ended, the Tigers were practically annihilated as a fighting force. (A. C. Bosselman & Co., #13007; c. 1910.)

Charge of the Louisiana Tiger's
Second Day's Battle, Gettysburg,
Pa.

GETTYSBURG, Pa. Spangler's Spring.

Spangler's Spring, actually two springs, is located at the base of Culp's Hill. This source of cool, clean water was utilized by both armies. Union soldiers held possession of these waters until the evening of July 2, when the Confederates captured the springs and the nearby breastworks without a fight. On the morning of the last day of battle, Union troops recaptured the area. Legend has it that the waters of Spangler's Spring were shared peacefully by soldiers of both armies during the evening of July 2. However, no evidence exists to support this traditional story. The granite structure seen in this postcard was constructed later to enclose the spring. (Raphael Tuck & Sons, ser. #2397; c. 1907.)

FOUR

DAY THREE

Culp's Hill, on the right flank of the Union's defensive line (the "fish hook"), was the scene of more fighting on the third day. During the night of July 2, General Greene's troops were reinforced by the remainder of the Union's 12th Corps. (W. H. Tipton, multiview set; *c.* 1905.)

OPPOSITE: At about 4:00 a.m. Confederate forces under General Johnson again attempted to dislodge the Union defenders. By 11:00 a.m. Union counter attacks successfully recaptured the breastworks and Spangler's Spring at the base of the hill. Confederate losses here would be almost as great as those suffered later during Pickett's Charge. (A. C. Bosselman & Co., #11716; *c.* 1910.)

Culp's Hill,
Gettysburg, Pa.

On the morning of July 3, one of the most poignant incidents of the battle occurred. Twenty-year-old Mary Virginia Wade, known as Jennie, was visiting her sister Mrs. McClellen. A bullet, believed to have been fired by a Confederate sniper, passed through two doors and struck her in the back as she baked bread for her family and Union soldiers. She died instantly, becoming the only recorded civilian fatality of the battle. (Raphael Tuck & Sons, ser. #2397; c. 1907.)

GETTYSBURG, PA.
The House in which Jennie Wade was killed and her Monument.

SCENE ON CONFEDERATE AVENUE, GETTYSBURG, PA.

Looking north from Pitzer's Woods along Confederate Avenue, cannons mark the position of Miller's Battery of the Washington Artillery from Louisiana. At 1:00 p.m. two guns from this battery fired in rapid succession to signal the start of the Confederates' great cannonade against the Union line in preparation for Pickett's Charge. Colonel Alexander, who was in charge of Lee's artillery, began a fierce bombardment that would last nearly two hours. (David Kaufman, #102499; c. 1920.)

Unsuccessful in his attempts to break the Union lines on the left and right, General Lee believed that a massive attack on the center was necessary. Against the advice of General Longstreet, Lee ordered three divisions totaling approximately 15,000 men led by Generals George Pickett, James Pettigrew, and Isaac Trimble to make the immortal assault. One of the most famous infantry charges in history, it resulted in almost 10,000 Confederate casualties. This picture depicting action during Pickett's Charge is the work of artist George Sacket and was first published in 1880. The Union 2nd Corps is shown defending the line while General Hancock courageously directs the Federal troops from horseback. It was here at the stone wall that the Confederate assault climaxed. Some historians believe the failure of this attack marked the turning point of the entire Civil War. (J. I. Mumper; 1909.)

Third Day's Battle–Pickett's Charge. Gettysburg, Pa.

BATTLE OF GETTYSBURG, GETTYSBURG, PA.

While the battle reached its apex at the center of the Union's defensive line during Pickett's Charge, intense fighting was taking place in other areas of the battlefield as well. In this scene from the famous Cyclorama painting, Lieutenant Cushing's battery is in action at the Bloody Angle. This key location, just to the right of the High Water Mark, received its name from the angle where two stone fences met. Behind the wall a battery commanded by Lt. Alonzo Cushing and infantry riflemen poured fire into the advancing rows of Confederates. It was at this spot that Confederate Gen. Lewis A. Armistead, his hat atop his sword, led 150 of his men over the stone wall. Armistead fell, mortally wounded, as he reached the guns of Cushing's battery. During hand-to-hand combat, most of his men were also killed or captured. (David Kaufman, #102526; c. 1920.)

Depicted in this picture is one of the most dramatic incidents of the third day's battle. The hero of the Bloody Angle, Lt. Alonzo Cushing, was killed while firing his last functioning cannon directly into the advancing enemy as they were about to overrun his position. His brave sacrifice helped break up the assault and turn the engagement into a Union victory. (A. C. Bosselman & Co., #13008; c. 1910.)

Death of Lieutenant Cushing at Bloody Angle, Gettysburg, Pa.

The largest cavalry engagement of the battle occurred across farm fields nearly three miles east of town when Confederate Gen. Jeb Stuart's 7,000 cavalrymen engaged in combat with 5,000 Union horsemen. Stuart was attempting to turn the Union right flank and attack Meade from the rear. Charges and countercharges continued throughout the afternoon until the Confederate cavalry, low on ammunition and having suffered heavy losses, were forced to retreat. (Interstate News Co., #G-43; c. 1910.)

ON EAST CAVALRY FIELD, GETTYSBURG, PA.

The Cavalry Battle, Gettysburg, Pa.

Illustrated here is a scene from the great cavalry battle that took place east of Gettysburg. In this incident Gen. Armstrong Custer, age 23, led the 1st Michigan Brigade in a charge against Gen. Wade Hampton's Brigade. Shouting "come on you wolverines," Custer inspired his men as they crashed into the Confederate ranks. The fighting became so violent that it has been referred to as "the saber fight." (J. I. Mumper; 1909.)

As one of the last actions of the battle, Union Gen. Judson Kilpatrick ordered a cavalry attack against General Longstreet's right flank near Big Round Top. Despite objecting strenuously to his commander about the futility of his orders, Gen. Elon J. Farnsworth nevertheless led the 1st West Virginia Cavalry in the assault. After being struck by five bullets, Farnsworth died fulfilling his duty. After three days of battle, General Lee realized that the Union forces would not counterattack and began his retreat back to the South. At Williamsport, Maryland, the Army of Northern Virginia successfully withdrew across the Potomac River on July 14. Even though Gettysburg was General Lee's last offensive campaign, the war continued for two more agonizing years. (M.A.P. Co., ser. 813; c. 1912.)

FARNSWORTH'S CHARGE
GETTYSBURG.

SERIES 813

FIVE

HALLOWED GROUND

A few days after the battle, Pennsylvania governor A. G. Curtin appointed prominent attorney David Wills to begin the establishment of a cemetery. Wills selected 17 acres at the highest point on Cemetery Hill to serve as the final resting place for those who fell in battle. Soldiers' National Cemetery was the first in the United States dedicated exclusively to the burial of soldiers. Pictured here is the eastern gate that opens onto Baltimore Pike. Dedicated on November 19, 1863, the cemetery was formally turned over to the federal government as a national cemetery on May 1, 1872. An iron fence separates this burial ground from the neighboring civilian Evergreen Cemetery. (Rotograph Co., #3719; 1904.)

On November 19, 1863, President Abraham Lincoln took part in the dedication ceremonies for the National Cemetery. Following a two-hour speech by famed orator Edward Everett, Lincoln rose to deliver his remarks, which lasted just over two minutes. Afterward, Lincoln was disappointed with his presentation and felt it to be inadequate. History, however, proved otherwise. (M. W. Taggart, series #606; 1908.)

OPPOSITE: Erected in 1814 at York Street on the square, this was the home of David Wills, who invited Lincoln to come to Gettysburg for the dedication ceremonies. Lincoln put the finishing touches on his speech, the "Gettysburg Address," while staying here. (C. T. Photochrom, #R-37843; c. 1913.)

LINCOLN DELIVERING HIS FAMOUS ADDRESS AT THE DEDICATION OF GETTYSBURG CEMETERY NOV 19 1863

The Wills House, where Lincoln wrote his
Gettysburg Address, Gettysburg, Pa.

AVENUE IN NATIONAL CEMETERY,

94

On this postcard from the early 1900s visitors stroll leisurely along one of the two tree-lined avenues running the length of the cemetery. The two cannon on the right mark the location of a Union artillery battery that was positioned here during the battle. It is almost possible to forget that this peaceful locale was once the scene of combat. (Rotograph Co., #E-3701a; c. 1907.)

Gettysburg, Soldier's National Cemetery

David Wills commissioned William Saunders, an eminent landscape gardener for the U.S. Department of Agriculture, to plan and design the layout of the cemetery. Each of the 18 Northern states that took part in the battle contributed to the costs. Saunders laid out the burial plots in a semicircular fashion with the dead arranged in parallel rows. There are 22 different sections. Each of the 18 Union states was assigned its own area; one section was reserved for U.S. Regular Army dead and three were devoted to the graves of the unknown. (Hugh C. Leighton, #5697; c. 1908.)

Great care was taken to identify the bodies of the dead when they were removed from the battlefield and during reinterment. However, due to the nature of the fighting and the identification techniques of the time, many remained unidentifiable. Today 1,664 bodies of those who fell in battle remain unnamed. Of the unknown, some 979 remain unidentifiable even as to their state military unit. These rows of small, uniformly sized stone markers record the final resting place for these fallen soldiers. (Excelsior, #B-4588; c. 1910.)

Graves of the Unknown Dead in The Soldiers' National Cemetery, Gettysburg, Pa.

SOLDIERS NATIONAL MONUMENT,
GETTYSBURG BATTLEFIELD, PA.

100

Standing near the spot where Lincoln gave his famous address, the Soldiers' National Monument was the first memorial of any kind to be placed at Gettysburg. The cornerstone was laid on July 4, 1865. Positioned at the center of the semicircle of gravesites, this monument stands as a tribute to all who fought here. Standing 60 feet high, its 25-foot-square pedestal accommodates four marble statues. The statues sculpted by Randolph Rogers symbolize "War," "History," "Peace," and "Plenty," while the statue on top is the "Genius of Liberty." General Meade, "the Victor of Gettysburg," was among the dignitaries who spoke at the dedication ceremonies on July 1, 1869. (Union News Co., #1155; c. 1910.)

SIX

IN REMEMBRANCE

On the edge of Spangler's Meadow is a small granite marker placed in memory of the men of the 2nd Massachusetts Infantry. It was here that some 316 men of that regiment made a courageous but unsuccessful charge across the field. Dedicated in May of 1879, this was the first regimental monument of any kind on the battlefield. Since then, nearly 1,400 monuments, memorials, markers, and tablets have been placed around the battlefield to pay tribute to those who fought here. On the back of the 2nd Massachusetts Infantry memorial is a plaque listing the names of all 45 men from the unit who died in the engagement. (Louis Kaufman & Sons, #12; *c.* 1907.)

Summit of Little Round Top, Gettysburg, Pa.

General Warren, the "Savior of Little Round Top," is memorialized by this bronze statue, which stands forever gazing out from the summit of Little Round Top. As chief engineer of the Army of the Potomac, it was his timely decision to order the occupation of the heights of Little Round Top that saved this vital position for the Union army. (J. I. Mumper; 1909.)

Located near the High Water Mark on Hancock Avenue, this impressive monument honors units of the Regular U.S. Army who fought here. Although greatly outnumbered by the volunteer units, these professional soldiers greatly contributed to the outcome of the battle. They were engaged over all areas of the battlefield and took part in some of the bloodiest of the fighting. Standing 85 feet tall, the granite obelisk was dedicated on May 30, 1909, by President William Howard Taft. Around the base of the monument are four large plaques listing each of the regiments and their commanders who fought at Gettysburg. An unusual feature of this memorial is the large patio that allows visitors to walk around the pedestal. (Union News Co., #1130; c. 1910.)

A GENERAL VIEW OF THE NATIONAL CEMETERY, GETTYSBURG, PA.

Located at the famed Copse of Trees along Hancock Avenue, this memorial marks the site of the High Water Mark of the Confederacy. It was here that the assault by Pickett's, Pettigrew's, and Trimble's divisions on July 3 reached its zenith. The monument is in the form of a large open book propped up by pyramids of cannonballs. Upon the pages are inscribed the names of the various Confederate and Union forces that faced each other in deadly combat on that fateful afternoon. (Pub. unknown, *c.* 1900.)

High Water Mark, Gettysburg. Reached by "Reading" fast trains.

111

PENNA. MEMORIAL - GETTYSBURG, PA. MOUNT AIRY GRANITE

112

The largest and most impressive of the state memorials, the Pennsylvania Memorial on Hancock Avenue honors the 34,530 soldiers from the commonwealth who fought here. The largest contingent of Union forces at Gettysburg, the names of each individual from Pennsylvania is recorded on bronze tablets placed around the parapets and on the inner walls of the arches. The memorial was constructed in the form of a massive dome supported by four large arches standing on a parapet 84 feet square. On top of the dome stands a 21-foot-tall statue of the "Goddess of Victory and Peace" that was cast from the bronze of cannon actually used during the Civil War. (Real photo card; c. 1910.)

SEVEN

THE LATER YEARS

On April 30, 1884, the Gettysburg Battlefield Memorial Association was established by the Commonwealth of Pennsylvania to purchase portions of the battlefield and preserve it for future generations. An act of Congress in 1895 placed the park under the jurisdiction of the U.S. War Department until 1933, when it was transferred to the National Park Service. Thus the Gettysburg National Military Park was brought into existence. (Koelling & Klappenbach, #59; c. 1904.)

In 1895 the government erected five steel observation towers at strategic points to allow visitors to look out over the battlefield, but today only two and a half remain. Only half of this tower on Oak Ridge still stands. To its left is the unusual, granite "oak tree–shaped" monument to the 90th Pennsylvania Infantry Regiment. (Leighton & Valentine, #216930; c. 1913.)

OPPOSITE: One of the towers still in use is this one, located atop the summit of Culp's Hill. (A. C. Bosselman & Co., #11722; c. 1910.)

Observation Tower on Oak Ridge, Gettysburg, Pa.

216930

Summit of Culp's Hill, Gettysburg, Pa.

119

After the war, veterans returned to Gettysburg for three major reunions, the first of which was in 1888. The 50th reunion, which lasted from June 29 to July 6, 1913, saw an estimated 55,000 veterans attend. This group of New York Grand Army of the Republic veterans met with New Hampshire governor Samuel D. Felker at their campsite during the 50th reunion. Most of the thousands of returning ex-soldiers camped on the old battlegrounds, and the former combatants of both North and South met in peace and remembrance of those history-making days a half century earlier. The final reunion was in 1938, when 1,845 visited the battlefield. At that time their average age was 94 years. (Real photo card; 1913.)

Gov. Felker and Drum Corps at Gettysburg, July 1 to 4, 1913.

This real photo postcard shows what appears to be an early tour group posing atop Little Round Top with General Warren's statue behind them. Their guide (standing to the left) is possibly a veteran of the battle, as were many of the early guides. (Real photo card; c. 1908.)

Gettysburg, on First Day's Field.

Capt. James Long,
Special Tourist Guide.
Office: Eagle Hotel, Gettysburg, Pa.
N. B. Transportation furnished.
Long Distance and Local Phones.

Capt. James T. Long, a veteran of the battle, is shown leading an automobile tour of the battlefield. He is pointing out to the visitors the direction from which the Confederate army advanced on the first day of the battle. Captain Long was a leading battlefield guide for 20 years and the author of a very popular book, *The 16th Decisive Battle of the World—Gettysburg*. (Pub. unknown, #2779; c. 1908.)

Perched on top of the rocks of Devil's Den, these young men posed for a photograph where Confederate sharpshooters once practiced their deadly art. The site has always been popular among visitors. This real photo postcard is the work of W. H. Tipton of Gettysburg, who was one of the more prolific photographers of the battlefield and published many postcard views of the area. (W. H. Tipton, #9005; *c.* 1907.)